Locally known as Patwa, the Kwéyòl language comes from an influence of mainly French but also English, Spanish and African native languages. Having many similarties to other varieties of Creole, spoken in countries such as, Haiti, Martinique and Guadeloupe, this strand of Creole is mainly spoken in the sister islands of Saint Lucia and Dominica.

This series of books seeks to preserve the deep cultural essence of the Kwéyòl language and it's influence for furture generations. Within this book you will find the Kwéyòl term for the parts of the body and the English translation. Each page includes an image to develop you and your family's use of Kwéyòl.

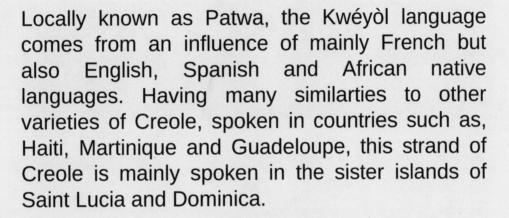

The body

Kò-a

Forehead

Fon

Hair

Chivé

Eyebrow

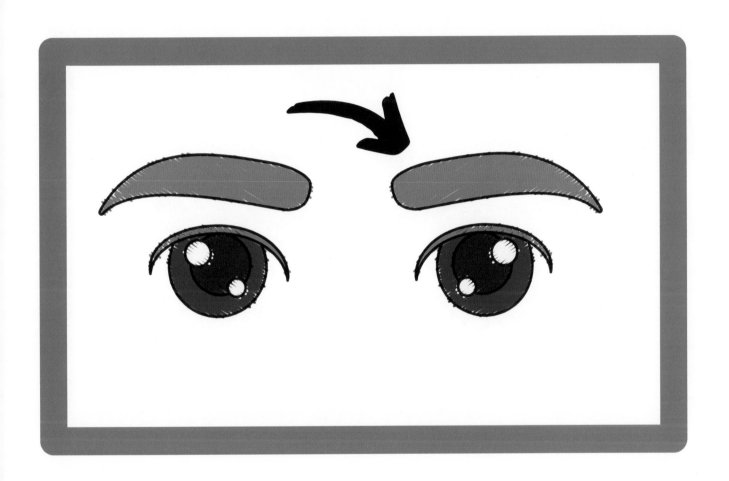

Sousi zyé

Eyelid

Lapo zyé

Face

Fidji

Eye

Zyé

Head

Tèt

Nose

Né

Ear

Zòwèyé

Teeth

Dan

Mouth

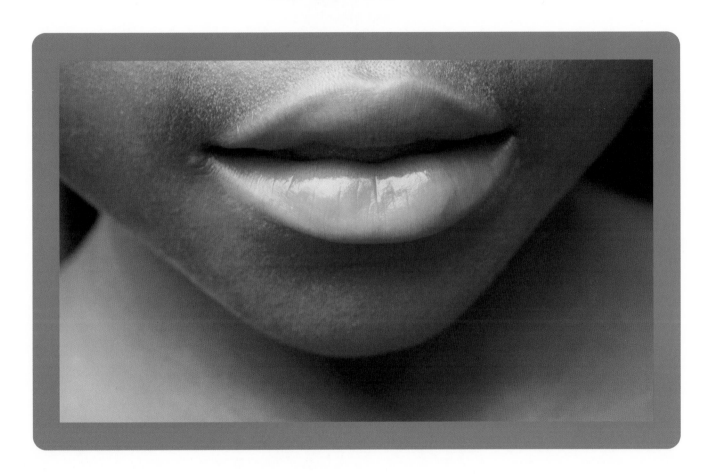

Bouch

Tongue

Lanng

Lip

Lèv

Chin

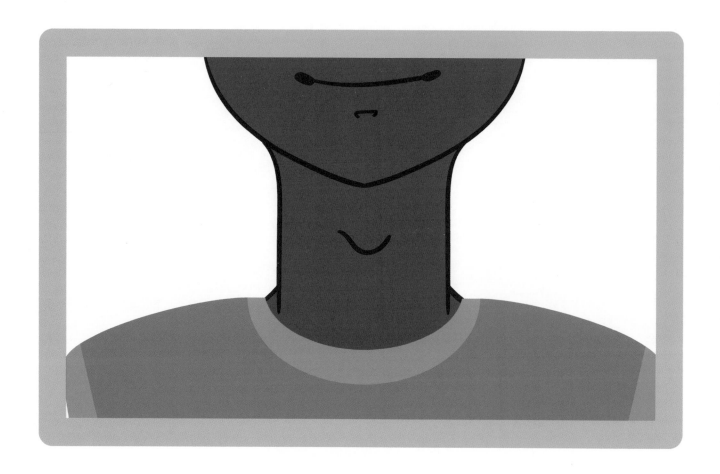

Maton

Throat

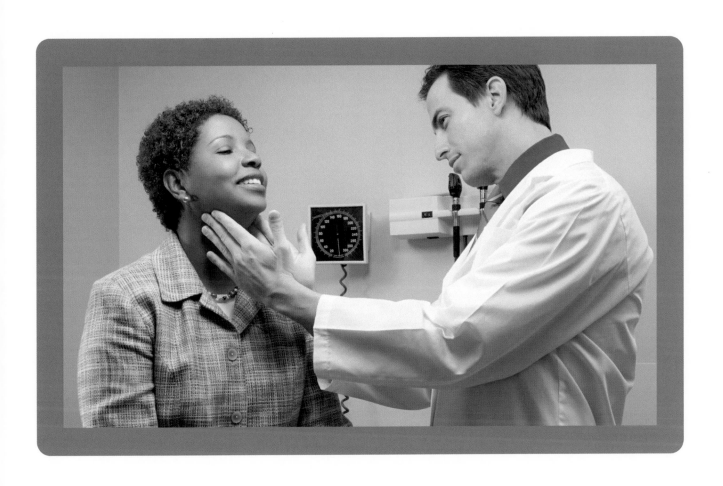

Gòj

Shoulder

Zépòl

Chest

Lèstomak

Arm

Bwa

Elbow

Koudbwa

Stomach

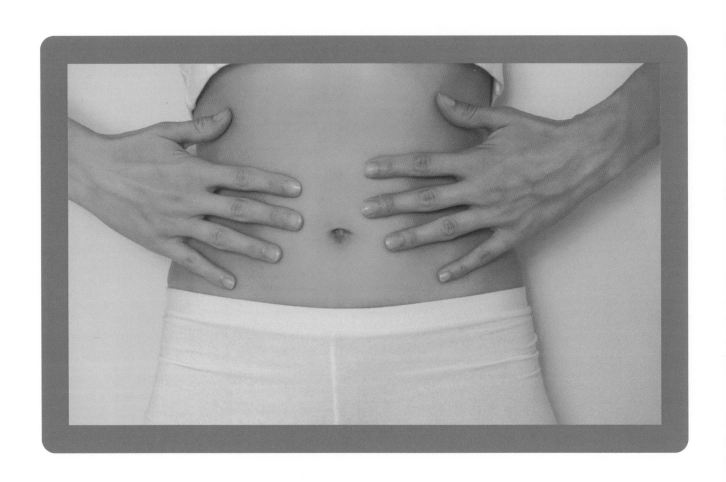

Bouden

Wrist

Ponyèt

Finger

Dwèt

Nail

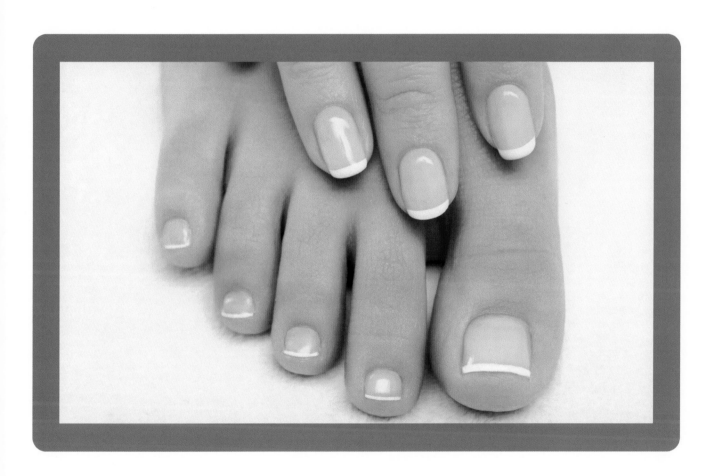

Zonng

Thumb

Gwo pous

Hand

Lamen

Waist

Wen

Hip

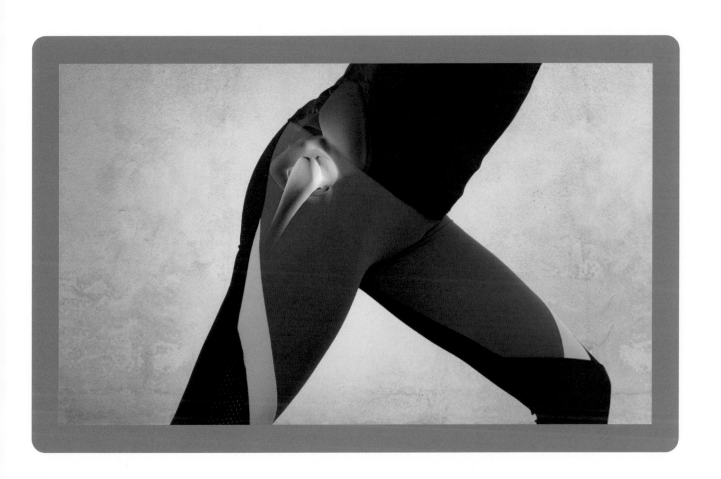

Hanch

Back

Do

Bottom

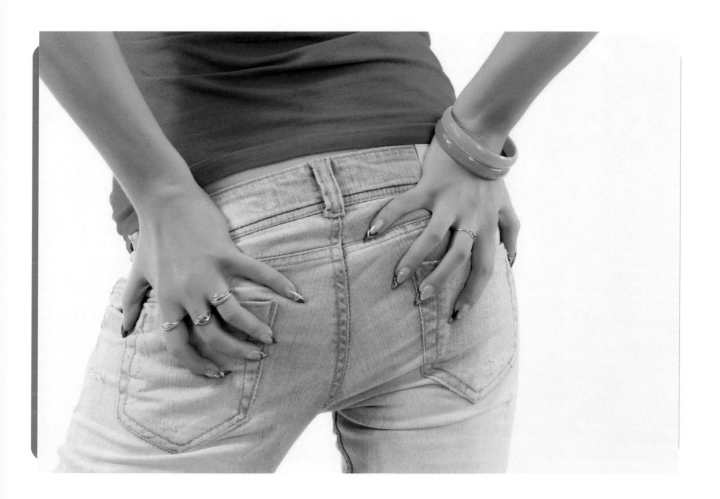

Fès

Leg

Janm

Knee

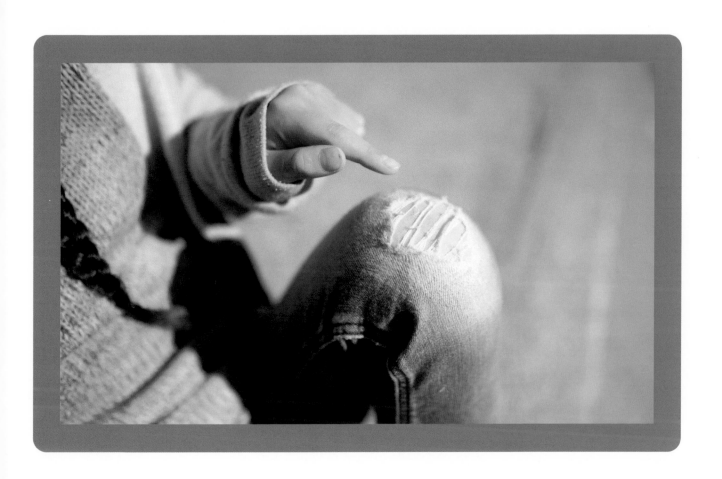

Jounou

Ankle

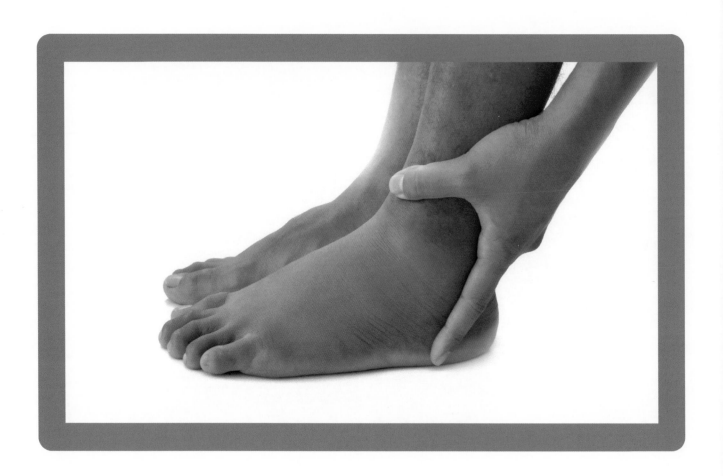

Chivi

Heel

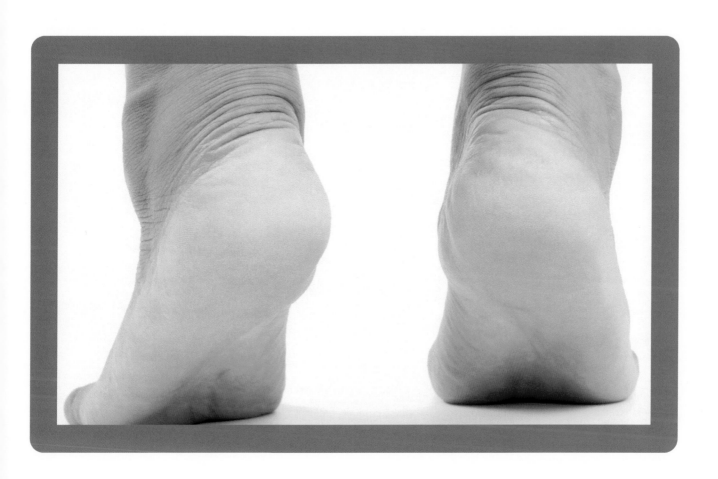

Talon

Foot

Pyé

Toe

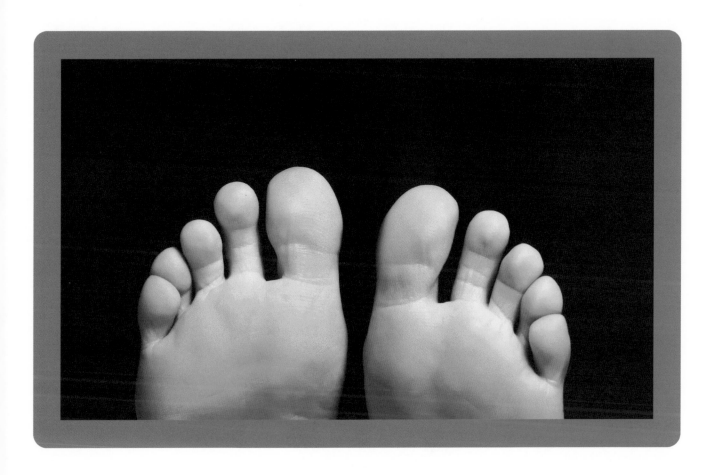

Zòtèy

Other books in this series:

More books coming soon

Printed in Great Britain
by Amazon